DISCIPLINE

WHAT IT REALLY TAKES TO BUILD
A SEVEN-FIGURE BUSINESS

ALI HEMYARI

FOUNDER, NASHVILLE K-9

DISCIPLINE

WHAT IT REALLY TAKES TO BUILD
A SEVEN-FIGURE BUSINESS

ALI HEMYARI

FOUNDER, NASHVILLE K-9

Copyright ©2024 HFC Holdings LLC.

All rights reserved. No part of this book may be reproduced or transmitted in any form or by any means, electronic or mechanical, including photocopying, recording, or by any information storage and retrieval system without written permission of the publisher, except for the inclusion of brief quotations in a review.

An Honorée Corder Bespoke Book Production

Designed by Dino Marino, www.dinomarinodesign.com.

E-book ISBN: 979-8-9893794-0-8

Paperback ISBN: 979-8-9893794-1-5

Hardcover ISBN: 979-8-9893794-2-2

DEDICATION

With the deepest love, this book is dedicated to my wife, son, and daughter. This book would not have existed without you.

To my mom: You're my hero. To my father: I would've been a terrible doctor—people would have died. To my brother: thanks for kicking me in the face more than once.

To the readers: I hope this is the shove you need to take action now.

To Dary: With a special thank you for building multiple facilities for us.

CONTENTS

PART III: SCALING FOR GROWTH

SPECIAL INVITATION

Be sure to sign-up for instant access
to all of the resources in this book,
including the Discipline Action Guide:
NashvilleK9.com/Discipline.

INTRODUCTION

So, you want to be a millionaire?

Great! Super easy, right?

According to lots of "influencers" and "experts," all you need to do is listen to countless podcasts, watch a bunch of YouTube videos, or read a few books on how to build a successful business.

You might find some good ideas, but there are three problems with this approach.

First, you'll hear a lot of conflicting advice. Many would-be entrepreneurs give up before they even get started because they're listening to too many different voices.

Second, those content creators are great at telling you what to do, but most of them haven't built a successful business themselves. Creating a seven-figure business is not about ideas and theory. It's about doing the work and taking action.

Third, the vast majority of those "influencers" leave out the most important factor that determines whether you will build a seven-figure business: *discipline*.

The word *discipline* sends shudders down the spine of everyone who wants a quick and easy path to success. But I'm here to tell you that it's anything but quick and easy. Success requires grit, determination, focus, action, and plain old hard work.

It doesn't matter what type of business you want to create. Maybe you're interested in construction, event planning, consulting, landscaping, IT, or another industry. Maybe you're in the dog training business like me.

Whatever the case, I'm here to give you a clear blueprint you can follow in building your own seven-figure empire. As the founder and owner of Nashville K-9, the most successful dog training facility in Middle Tennessee, I've put in years of effort and discipline. I'm honored to show you the way.

WHO THIS BOOK IS FOR

I've written *Discipline* for two types of people.

First, it's for anyone who wants to get started building their own business. You might be twenty-six, seventy-six, or somewhere in between, but you've always dreamed of owning a business and taking control of your destiny.

Second, this book is for people in the corporate world who are tired of the rat race. You're sick of being controlled by someone else's schedule. You don't want false limits placed on your success or income.

Regardless of why you came to this book, I promise to do my best to make the process of growing your own business simple and doable if you're willing to put in the sweat equity and be disciplined.

Here's a quick road map of what's ahead.

In Part One, I'll lay the foundation for creating a business. You'll learn about the six pillars of business and why they're critical. I'll share why educating yourself, marketing, and investing in your business are also important pieces of your success.

We'll continue in Part Two by talking about how to work with clients. Your business cannot exist without clients and customers. You'll learn how to sell your services, do the actual work you've promised, and teach the client what they need to know for success.

Then, in Part Three, you will learn how to scale your business for growth. This includes following up with clients and reinvesting your profits. We'll close by exploring what it means to build your business so you can eventually sell it.

Building a business doesn't need to be complicated. As you can see, there's a clear step-by-step pathway I've laid out for you. The real issue is sticking with your business over the long haul.

The process I've laid out is *simple*, but I didn't say it was *easy*. Au contraire! There are times when you will want to quit. You'll make mistakes you regret. At times, you'll wonder whether it's worth it.

But if you stick with it and you keep growing and learning, you'll be so glad you did.

You're probably wondering how I came to learn these lessons myself. Let me give you a snapshot of where I've come from and why this book is so important to me.

MY STORY

I was always drawn to entrepreneurship. My family and I are first-generation immigrants. During the revolution in Iran, my parents wanted to escape a radical religious government, and we went through the process of becoming US citizens.

We left everything in Iran, including family and friends, to start all over again in the United States. My mom didn't even speak English. Even though that journey was financially challenging for us, I knew when I grew up that I wanted the American dream. Only in the greatest country in the world could you create opportunity as long as there was demand.

I didn't waste any time. As a college student (go Vols!) in the late 1990s and early 2000s, I started several businesses, including Highline

Exotics (brokering exotic cars), University Marketing Consultants (a full-service advertising company), and SociEvent (an event planning company catered toward fraternities and sororities). Also, while in college, I had a hobby and passion for training dogs as a member of a working dog club (Tennessee Valley DVG Schutzhund—Sandy and Ron Pope).

I came back to Nashville in 2005 and worked for AXA Financial as a pre-contract financial advisor. From there, I jumped into residential and commercial lending. I started Nashville K-9 in 2005 as a working dog group and focused my training on police dogs, protection dogs, and search and rescue. I learned that training dogs could be a viable business.

Over the next few years, I either joined or started the K-9 teams of several local municipalities. Part of this was to benefit my community. The other part of this was to benefit my business. I went through my first Special Weapons and Tactics (SWAT) K-9 school in 2009. The following year, I became a commissioned law enforcement officer and began flight school, earning my fixed-wing pilot's license in 2011. A couple of years later, I became a helicopter pilot.

A few years after that, I earned my high-performance airplane rating. Even though it was my dream and a challenge to become a pilot, I was also able to interface with ultra-high-net-worth people in the aviation industry. I'd bump into unique people at airports, begin conversations, and establish relationships. That turned prospects into clients.

From 2012 to 2018, I was busy growing Nashville K-9 and becoming a more well-versed law enforcement officer. Becoming a police officer allowed me to sell more dogs to municipalities. But more importantly, it allowed me to understand what they went through and needed. I became a Peace Officer Standards and Training (POST) Commission certified Law Enforcement Firearms Instructor (LEFI), SWAT operator, and SWAT sniper.

I was also able to continue increasing my philanthropy. I've donated thousands of hours in police work, search and rescue, as an ambassador to different non-profits, as well as serving on the Board of Directors for Make-

A-Wish and many other charities. I'm still an active police officer at no charge to taxpayers.

One of my personal highlights was collaborating with my Nashville K-9 client Kelly Clarkson to donate a dog to Abe's Garden (an Alzheimer's residence facility). Over the years, we've donated many dogs to police departments, people in need, and other organizations—even unique dogs that specialize in electronics detection, Parkinson's service, or peanut detection.

In the last few years, Nashville K-9 has hit a number of milestones, including acquiring our first jet (a 1995 Hawker 800XP), expanding our training facility in Franklin, and launching Pawdentity (point-of-sale software that also optimizes kennel management for pet resorts, trainers, veterinarians, animal control, and more).

I was inducted into *Nashville Business Journal's* Top 40 Under 40 in 2021 and *Marquis Who's Who in America*. The following year, we were featured on Bloomberg as the "World's Greatest Canine Training Facility."

I don't say any of this to brag. I just want to make it clear that I'm not a guy speaking from theory. I've done the work and built my business from the ground up. It took *discipline*.

But I haven't done it alone. I've had plenty of help and support from my team members, community, those who have trained me, and, of course, my wife and two children.

Most important, I couldn't have done any of this without God's help. He's helped me every step of the way. I'm not anywhere close to a saint, and I've made many mistakes, but I do try to live my life like Jesus as best I can.

I believe that success can only be achieved by believing in, knowing, and loving God. Saint Augustine famously said, "Pray like it all depends on God, and work like it all depends on you."

I'll leave the faith part up to you and will do my best to help you do the work.

WHAT'S YOUR STORY?

You've heard some of *my* story. What about *yours*?

In every great story, there is a compelling villain who wants to stop the hero from achieving their goal. In this case, the villains are three lies that will keep you from building a great business.

LIE ONE: THIS IS GOING TO BE EASY.

You might look at my large, successful business or my private jet and think, *That's the kind of life I want!* And I wouldn't blame you. I have a great life!

I've laid out a clear pathway for you to follow in this book, but it's not going to be a cakewalk. No, this journey is going to take a lot of discipline and sacrifice. You'll have late nights and early mornings. If you want this kind of life, you've got to put in the work.

LIE TWO: SCHOOL IS GOING TO TEACH YOU EVERYTHING YOU NEED TO KNOW.

Don't get me wrong, college has its place in the world. But for the most part, professors who are teaching business just have an MBA and haven't built a successful business themselves.

Business is more than running graphs and Venn diagrams. Where do you get a business license? How do you form an LLC? How do you build relationships with your community? You probably won't learn any of those things in a classroom.

LIE THREE: YOUR DESTINY IS ALREADY DETERMINED.

Some people quit before they even get started. They think, *I'm not wired to be an entrepreneur* or *I'm not a hard-charging assertive type.* It doesn't matter. You can rewire yourself.

Just like a night owl can rewire themselves into a morning person, you can become a successful business owner. You can break old habits and form new ones.

Easy? No. Possible? Absolutely.

We'll talk more about false beliefs later in the book. For now, I want you to be on the lookout for these subtle lies that derail a lot of potentially great entrepreneurs.

Let's get started with the foundation: the Six Pillars of Business.

PART I

BUILDING THE FOUNDATION

CHAPTER ONE

UNDERSTAND THE SIX PILLARS OF BUSINESS

If you travel to Greece, it's impossible not to notice its most famous building, the Parthenon. This ancient temple to the Greek goddess Athena was built around 2,500 years ago on the highest point of Athens—a rocky outcropping known as the Acropolis (literally "high city").

The most striking part of the Parthenon is its columns. Like the rest of the building, they're built from white Pentelic marble. The columns aren't just functional. They also symbolize power, strength, and longevity.

The Parthenon has been around ten times longer than the United States has been a nation. It will last many thousands of years into the future.

In fact, the Parthenon is such an iconic piece of architecture that we have a full-size replica of it right here in Nashville!

Without strong pillars, the Parthenon wouldn't stay standing. The same is true for your business. It has to be built on timeless principles that will help you last over the long haul.

The six pillars I'm sharing in this chapter are going to build your wealth. It's not easy to make a million dollars. There's no magic potion you can drink, and *poof*, you have a seven-figure business.

But if you follow these principles and work on your mindset, you can be a millionaire in a relatively short amount of time. Even if you only apply half of them, you'll still be successful.

PILLAR ONE: BE RESPONSIVE

When someone sends you an email or leaves a voice message or text message, respond back as soon as you can. It's that simple. When you delay, it indicates to the other person that they're not important.

One of the most frustrating things I hear are voice messages saying, "Please leave your name and a brief message, and I'll call you back at my earliest convenience." It tells people that *your* time is more valuable than theirs.

If you want to build a business, your potential partner, client, or customer needs to know *their* time is important. They want to feel valued.

When you fail to do this, you will disappoint people, and they will not want to continue doing business with you or perhaps not buy from you in the first place.

Here's a recent example. I have my suits custom-made by a well-known clothier. You would think that a high-end clothier would give you service equal to their reputation. But that hasn't been the case. I've had issues with the last six suits they've made for me.

As of this writing (September 2023), I've been working on resolving this issue since the previous December—almost an entire year. It's still not fixed.

Soon after I started having problems, I called them and said, "I'll come to you. I'd like to see your tailor so I can get the fitting issues resolved."

They said, "Here are the times the tailor is available." I drove to the store, but the tailor wasn't there.

I recently went back into the store to try yet again, and my sales guy wasn't there. Neither was the tailor. I told the office manager, "Listen, these are custom suits, not off-the-rack garments. I've spent a good deal of money on these. They are supposed to be designed for my body. I expect better service than this. My salesperson isn't here, and neither is the tailor. This is a problem."

No matter what the specific business, this type of thing is a consistent issue in the sales industry overall. Nearly everyone is playing the game of mediocrity today.

That's no way to win in business. Be responsive and make it clear to people that they are important to you.

PILLAR TWO: BE RELIABLE & HONEST

If you tell somebody you're going to do something, it's your obligation to do it.

If you tell someone, "I'm going to meet you for lunch at 12:00 p.m.," don't show up at 12:15 p.m. That's not reliable. If you're supposed to clock in at work by 8:00 a.m., be there by 7:55 a.m. Don't show up at 8:05 a.m. and expect people to think you're dependable.

In the dog training world, if you tell someone, "I'm going to train your dog to sit," the dog should be able to sit.

It's not easy to be reliable and honest. Sometimes, it will cost you. Literally.

A couple of years ago, I sold my Terradyne Gurkha truck. The Gurkha is a very rare and extremely valuable armored vehicle. We used it for business for a little while, but I wanted to put it on the market.

A gentleman from Florida contacted me and said he wanted to buy it. He flew up from Florida, gave me a $1,000 deposit, shook my hand, and left with the intention of finishing the deal.

Soon after he left, I started getting calls from people offering me up to $40,000 more than he did. Part of me considered giving the guy his $1,000 back and selling it to a buyer willing to pay more.

But I had shaken his hand, and we made a deal that I chose to honor. A year later, I heard that he sold the truck for $130,000 more than what he paid me for it.

That was a little painful to hear, but I could sleep at night because I was honorable and kept my word. Your reputation is worth more than a few dollars.

That's the example I want to set for my kids and employees.

PILLAR THREE: WORK HARDER THAN ANYONE ELSE YOU KNOW

When I started Nashville K-9 as a side hustle, I still worked in the banking world as a lender for residential and commercial loans.

I would wake up early to train and run the dogs, go back home to shave and shower, and then go to work. I'd work at my banking job, and then in the middle of the day, I'd skip lunch to go to the gym and get my workout in.

I'd come back to my desk and eat lunch while I was working. Then, I would go home to train and exercise the dogs. I'm not talking about one or two dogs. It was eight to ten dogs at a time. It was difficult.

I bought a Chevy Tahoe that had a police cage in it for dogs. I'd have four dogs in the car. I'd train them all individually, one at a time. I'd allow them to exercise, then put them all back into the vehicle and go home. I'd take out the dogs and load up another four, go back out to train them, and then bring them back to the house.

I'd feed and water the dogs, take a quick shower, then jump back into my work clothes and stay at work until 7:30 p.m. or 8:00 p.m. I'd work on lending and make cold calls to people because that's when they were home. These were the days when Bluetooth was in its infancy, so I had to make calls from work.

After work, I'd go home and let the dogs out to repeat the whole routine. Then I'd shower again, go to sleep, and rinse and repeat the next day. This went on for so many years that it became a habit.

It's hard to motivate yourself in the morning when you're headed into pouring rain, freezing snow, or ninety-degree heat. But the dogs are counting on you to do it.

On the weekends, I would work on loans and catch up on paperwork. In the midst of all that, I would also go to churches, schools, and other organizations for dog events and demonstrations.

My whole life, seven days a week, was focused on working. As a single man, on Friday and Saturday nights, I'd go out to the bars and restaurants with my buddies and let loose a little bit.

But the next morning, even if I was exhausted from the lack of sleep and the hustle and bustle of the week, I'd still be out there training the dogs and getting the work done. That was on top of lending and doing police work.

Those years of putting in the constant work taught me a valuable lesson: you must have a "whatever it takes" mentality. It's especially important when you're in your twenties and have more time, particularly if you're single and don't have kids. You've got to be willing to take action.

I can't impress upon you enough that some of the magic of building a successful business is putting in the work prior to having kids or being married. This gives you the ability to work longer and harder and take risks that are much more difficult when you are married, especially if you have children.

My wife has lived with me through four house moves in four years, all for Nashville K-9. She was with me in my townhome with eight dogs. In the second house, we used the garage for kennel crates. In the third one, we converted the garage to cinderblock kennels. The fourth move was to a farm.

Her whole family helped me epoxy paint the cinderblock kennels. *They* were invested in seeing me be successful. *They* cared.

Who you marry matters. I have friends whose wives are quick to complain, get negative, don't want to sacrifice, and don't want to help.

You will not be a successful entrepreneur if this is the spouse you choose.

I fielded phone calls seven days a week, early mornings and late evenings, all with my supportive wife cheering me on. I rinsed dozens of kennel crates outside in subfreezing weather in lieu of going out to a nice dinner with my wife, and she was supportive throughout. She supports and helps me to this day.

Having a supportive partner gives you the time and energy to work longer and harder and take risks that are much more difficult when you are married. Especially if you have children.

It doesn't matter what your business is. Every successful person I've met has the mentality that you've got to do whatever it takes to get the job done. It requires commitment and discipline.

PILLAR FOUR: HAVE GENUINE GRATITUDE

We have baked gratitude into everything we do at Nashville K-9. Every one of my staff is trained to say some variation of "Thank you for the opportunity," or "Thank you for choosing Nashville K-9," to every single client when they're dropping off their dog, during the training process, and at pickup.

We've made it a part of our culture. We all understand that our livelihoods are dependent on each person who chooses us to train their dog. That person has bypassed 150 other trainers to come to us. We owe them a debt of gratitude.

This "attitude of gratitude" enables you to be much more successful in business because you sincerely appreciate customers and clients for choosing you.

I recently hosted a fundraiser where we raised over $180,000 for charity. This money came mostly from my clients. Why were they willing to give and participate? Because they saw Nashville K-9's gratitude for their business.

Handwritten notes have become a lost art in most corners of business, but not in my corner. We send tons of thank-you notes and cards.

Cards go a lot further than emails. I'm not saying we shouldn't use the phone or email. Of course, we should. But a card in the mail takes more effort and time. People notice.

Guess what happens? They come back to you when they need you to board or train their dog. They also come back when they have questions because they know you're sincere. That continual relationship can lead to repeat business and more referrals.

Luxury brands get it. When you buy a Ferrari, they roll out the red carpet and send you home with a bunch of swag. They make phone calls to you and send you to exclusive events. You'll get surprise black boxes with gifts.

But why does it have to be the high-end exclusive brands who only do this?

You can make the same kind of impression on customers no matter what your business or how big or small it is. Handwritten notes are a fantastic and inexpensive way to do this.

Dale Carnegie said it best in his classic book *How to Win Friends and Influence People*: "Become genuinely interested in other people." It doesn't mean you have to become best friends with everyone. It just means that your relationship isn't purely transactional. You appreciate them and are thinking about them.

Everybody wants to feel important. After all, a person's name is the sweetest sound they will hear!

But you can go beyond notes, calls, and emails for those extra special clients. For those who spend a certain amount of money with us each year, we go above and beyond. We reward them by painting a custom image of their dog on our wall.

This tells the client, "You've let us become a part of your life by allowing us to train your dog. Now, we want to make you part of ours."

You wouldn't believe how people respond to this simple gesture. For example, we trained a sheriff's office dog for therapy, and we did a painting of the dog with a little badge. The client was over the moon.

Whatever your business, you can find unique and special ways to make sure people know you appreciate them.

PILLAR FIVE: TAKE CARE OF YOUR COMMUNITY

I joined Nashville's Rescue Squad in 2006 and ran an all-volunteer search and rescue unit for the city. Every time little Timmy went missing, or someone was suspected of taking their own life, people had to go look for them and, in some cases, recover the body.

I did that at no charge. It's all completely voluntary, and I still run that team to this day.

Since I became a police officer, I have never once taken a paycheck. Whenever I did get some pay here and there, I would donate it to a flower fund or back to the department itself.

In addition to serving in those capacities, I've joined boards for organizations such as the Make-A-Wish Foundation and sponsored many charitable events.

Successful people feel a deep obligation to give back to their communities and steward their gifts. While it's not 100 percent altruistic because you can develop business relationships, that's not the point. Any business benefits are a bonus because the goal is to be generous and philanthropic.

These kinds of efforts also honor God. I consider philanthropy part of the giving process. You can tithe in many different ways.

Giving financially to your church is just one of them.

Some people are so selfish that they believe they did it all on their own, with no help from God or others. I've been around a lot of really good business leaders who don't believe in God and are not philanthropic.

Yet, I've also been around many who do, and there's a difference. The ones who see giving and serving as part of their business generally thrive more profoundly than those who don't.

When you take care of your community, your community will take care of you. But it has to be genuine. You can't serve expecting to get something out of it. That's the wrong mentality.

When I die, I don't want to be known as the best dog trainer in the world or the guy who owned a bunch of businesses. I want to be known as a philanthropist, a good father, and a good husband.

PILLAR SIX: BUILD RELATIONSHIPS

There are two ways you can look at a business.

It can be transactional, which means you sell someone a widget and probably won't talk to them again until you have a new widget to sell them.

Or it can be relational, which means you befriend the person who bought your widget. It doesn't mean you need to have dinner with them or make them your best friend. But you are intentionally following up with them.

The dog training world can be very transactional. You train a dog, you move on, you train a dog, you move on. But if you're truly interested in the other person and how they're doing, you'll want to see how their dog is progressing. You're almost like an accountability partner.

You ask questions like

- How is your dog doing?
- What kinds of issues have you been running into?
- Do you have any questions I can answer?
- How can we get your family involved in your dog's ongoing training?

- Is there anything I can do to make your experience better?

Questions like these are a much better way to follow up than saying, "Here's your dog," and moving on to the next client. Follow-up is a critical part of building the relationship.

Sending cards is important, but so is consistent contact. Send them emails and texts and call them on the telephone. "Hi, so-and-so, I'm getting in touch to check up on you. There's no need to reply. I just wanted to let you know you're in my thoughts."

Maybe you don't get them on the line, or they may not reply, but they know you were checking in.

When you're consistent with building relationships, that can lead to a lot of loyalty and repeat business.

You see this a lot in the automotive industry, where people in their sixties and seventies are selling cars by appointment only. They've built up a portfolio of relationships they can depend on to keep bringing in business. They don't have to be grinding it out like younger people or rookies in the industry would have to do.

These sales guys can come into work and leave when they want yet are still top producers. They have earned the right over decades of building relationships.

You also see this in the title side of real estate. A title company thrives on having mortgage lenders and real estate agents send them business. The relationships they have with the agents and mortgage loan officers are imperative to their business because those individuals can always choose another title company.

If you want to be in business for the long haul, it's critical to build relationships that lead to loyalty.

THIS IS THE FOUNDATION

There you have it. These six pillars are the essential foundation for any type of business.

Can you create a business without these pillars? Of course. Many people do. But the vast majority of those businesses don't last because they're not built on a great foundation:

the character, discipline, and relationships that create long-term success.

Don't be like those people. Instead, choose these six pillars for your foundation so you can build a business that lasts over the long haul.

Now that we've laid the right foundation, let's move to the next element: educating yourself.

CHAPTER TWO

EDUCATE YOURSELF

"Education" is a dirty word to most people.

For the masses, the word refers to a mandatory process that lasts for most of their early lives. From about ages five to eighteen, education means sitting through countless classes at a desk, occasionally escaping from the prison for lunch or recess.

Formal education lasts even longer if you go to college or grad school. Plus, you get the lovely added bonus of being deeply in debt for years to come.

I say that "education" is a dirty word because most people don't really enjoy it. They look at it as mostly pointless classes that don't teach many valuable skills. There's a huge amount of time and human potential wasted through formal education.

Entrepreneurs and business owners, on the other hand, look at education in a totally different light. It's not formal education that unlocks the door to business success.

The real secret is *self-education*. When you educate yourself about your industry and business, the whole world opens up to you.

There are only three ways in business to become a millionaire:

1. Someone gives you the money through an inheritance or the lottery.

2. You become a well-paid CEO or other corporate-type leader.

3. You build a successful business.

Since you're reading this book, I'm pretty sure I know which avenue you want to pursue. Now that you understand why the six pillars are important, you're ready to take the first step, which is being responsible for educating yourself.

KNOWING YOUR INDUSTRY

To be a true professional, you must know how to produce the results your industry delivers. In my world, you have to know the psychology behind dog training.

Let me give you a quick lesson.

There are two main theories that dictate human interaction. The first one is Pavlovian conditioning, also called classical conditioning. The second one is called operant conditioning.

Pavlovian conditioning is essentially pairing a neutral stimulus with the reward to get a conditioned response. While studying the digestive tracts of animals, Pavlov was ringing a bell, feeding dogs, ringing a bell, and feeding dogs. In the process, he noticed that when they heard the bell ring, it caused them to salivate because they were anticipating food.

The learning point here was that a neutral stimulus, paired with a reward, will produce a conditioned response.

Around the same time, another psychologist named Thorndike was studying reinforcement and punishment from both a positive and a negative perspective. B. F. Skinner took his work further and called it "operant conditioning."

Pavlov and Skinner were trying to prove human theories and interaction, but their subjects were animals, specifically canines. You'd be shocked at how many people in the dog training industry don't know the difference between positive punishment and negative reinforcement.

The preconceived notion is that *negative* means bad and *positive* means good. But that's not what it means. *Positive* means to have or to add, and *negative* means to withhold or take away. *Punishment* means decreasing the likelihood that a certain behavior will happen again. *Reinforcement* means you are increasing the likelihood that something will occur.

But generally, you hear dog trainers say, "I only use positive reinforcement." That's not possible because it doesn't fall into the framework that B. F. Skinner created.

Let's say you have a handful of rewards, and you ask a dog to sit, but he doesn't sit. You're not going to give him those treats since he wasn't listening when you asked him to sit. The mere act of withholding that reward is called *negative punishment*. In this context, *negative* just means that you're withholding something that the dog wants in order to get the desired result.

I'd estimate that 80 percent of dog trainers don't know that. But it's one of the fundamental pieces of knowledge you need to have as a professional dog trainer. You have to grasp and ultimately memorize these concepts if you want to be effective.

If you operate in a service-based industry, you have to understand how to do the work and do it well. Otherwise, you're not providing value. That's why it's critical to go to workshops and seminars, read books, and become educated in the fundamentals of your industry.

BECOMING A TOP PRODUCER

As important as the fundamentals are, they're not enough. If you want to rise to the top of your industry and build a seven-figure business, you've got to have the mindset of becoming a top producer.

Top producers constantly invest in their own training and education, while average producers do not.

Let's take the sales world, for example. If you work for a Fortune 500 company, they generally have their own internal sales curriculum where you can learn how to be a great salesperson. It will require you to understand all the nuances of sales, how to overcome objections, and how to maneuver around various conditions so you have a better chance of getting to "yes."

That is all well and good. You can go through training and still be a mediocre salesperson. Why? Because training won't fix the core issue, which is your motivation to become better.

Let's say you're shopping for a home theater system. Here's how a conversation with a great salesperson might go down:

"Hi there. What are you looking for?"

"I'm looking for a home theater system."

"Would you like Dolby Atmos? Maybe a THX system?"

"I really like the idea of Atmos. I'd also like to have some speakers in the ceiling."

"Are you talking about your living room, or do you have a custom home theater?"

At this point, you can tell the salesperson wants to go through the process with you. They have a good base of product knowledge and want to understand your needs. They can guide you effectively to the products that will work best while also staying within your budget.

The conversation continues:

"What kinds of media will you be using—mainly streaming, or will you also be using Blu-rays?"

"We'll mainly be streaming."

"What are you looking at spending?"

"I was thinking about something in the $10,000 range."

"Okay, you will need installation. Do you want to do it yourself?"

"No, I'd love to have someone take care of that for me."

This kind of attention to detail is what really makes you a sales professional. You're keeping the other person's interest piqued while also asking a variety of questions.

This type of salesperson is much better positioned to close the deal than the average salesperson. We've all had the experience of walking into an electronics store and asking where the TVs are located. A half-interested guy points to the back of the store and says, "Over there."

This is happening in every industry and at every level. Whether it's something as basic as going to a restaurant or picking up takeout, all the way to buying a major appliance or even a high-end vehicle, mediocrity in sales has become the norm.

Later in the book, I have a whole chapter on sales, but I mention it now because learning to sell must be part of your education. It's never too early to work on your sales skills. Without it, your business will be over before you even get started.

MENTORS CAN TAKE YOU FURTHER

Educating yourself is not only about what you can do. It's also about how others further along the journey can help you.

The president of the United States, no matter what their political affiliation, is always surrounded by a cabinet of advisors. These people inform the president about crucial matters and help them make decisions.

There's no such thing as a president who knows everything!

When you're starting off in business, you can build something like a cabinet of advisors by seeking out business mentors. I'd recommend that you seek out a few great mentors who can help with various aspects of your business.

I've had some great mentors, including Dustin David, Jackie and Chuck Cowden, Matthew Gelfand, my wife, and my good friends Jess and Damon Baba-Rahimi, to name a few. These are my personal friends and clients who have become family.

I've had amazing friends I consider teammates who have helped build the business: John Poland, Nick Wolkonsky, Raine Mitchell, and Katie Mason. They genuinely wanted me to succeed, and they helped me at every opportunity they could.

Find people who only want the best for you. While it may seem like those people are hard to find, there are some good ones out there.

If you're always hanging out with losers, you're going to be a loser. If you're hanging out with people who are doing better than you, they'll pull you up to their level. Those people will drive you.

Where can you find such mentors?

I would start by seeking out people in your field who might be willing to meet for lunch. Great business leaders are eager to help motivated people.

I'd also recommend getting involved in your local community's business organizations, such as Rotary, or groups and events where business leaders hang out. This is a great way to meet others and build relationships.

THE MAGIC OF RECURRING REVENUE

Before moving on to the next chapter, I want to highlight that it's important to not just learn about your industry, but about business itself.

Specifically, I encourage you to think about how to build recurring revenue into your business model. If you want to build a seven-figure business, you need to have products or services people will pay for over and over again.

In the early years of Nashville K-9, I would go to people's houses or meet them at the park to train their dogs. I remember one client with young kids who was busy in the mornings taking her kids to school.

She needed her dog exercised, so I'd drive to her house, pick up her dog, and go for a run. Then I'd return the dog.

I charged her forty dollars per day for this, and I was going for a run anyway. At the end of each week, I'd have two hundred dollars extra—basically money to reinvest in my business. That experience inspired me to start thinking of ways I could make more money from clients by providing more services or different versions of existing services.

Eventually, this led to the founding of a company called Pet Taxxi, where we take a client's dog to the vet and other locations for them. It's also why we got involved in aviation.

By having our own private jet, we could cater to clients who want to travel with their pets but can't take them on a conventional airline flight.

As you build your business, think about ways people can pay you regularly for your services, not just one time.

Check out my list of recommended reading in the back of this book and in this book's bonuses. You can get them at NashvilleK9.com/Discipline.

CHAPTER THREE

INVEST IN YOUR BUSINESS

Now that you have a desire to build a successful business, you understand the six pillars we've discussed, and you've started educating yourself about it, it's time to get down to brass tacks.

This is the part of building a business that's make or break. Why? Because now you're not just operating in theory; you're putting cold, hard cash and your precious time and energy into your dream.

In this chapter, we'll look at a few different places you'll need to invest as you build your seven-figure business.

BUSINESS NECESSITIES

The first thing you need to do is make sure that you have the proper business license from your city and state. Without it, you could be in a load of trouble down the line, particularly if you have a storefront or property.

And depending on the type of business you have, you will need to look into insurance as well. It's hard to give much more specific advice about this because every business and every location is different. But you must perform your due diligence so you're on the up and up.

I'd also recommend creating a business entity outside yourself so you decrease your personal liability. Whether that's an LLC, an S corp, or some other type of structure, I recommend you talk to a licensed business professional for specific advice.

The same goes for hiring people like an accountant, attorney, and so on. Your needs will be different according to your type of business.

My main point is that you should approach your business as a true professional.

Some people want to avoid all these headaches and just "get started." But if you don't begin with the proper licenses, structure, and insurance, you're putting yourself and your family at great risk.

You also need to think about all the physical assets you'll need to conduct your business and serve your clients. For example, if you have a dog training business, you'll need food and water, a vehicle, leashes, collars, kennels, a computer, and a phone, just to name a few things.

And in order to appear professional, I'd also recommend getting some swag with your logo in addition to wearing a uniform with the same logo. Your appearance makes a big difference. (More on that later.)

If you're not sure where to start, do some research on your industry, and it won't take long to figure out the assets and materials you need.

YOUR WEBSITE

I can't emphasize enough how important it is to have a good website and keep it updated. I'm shocked at how many people have websites that look like they were built in 1997, with links that are broken and information that's out of date.

What an imprudent mistake to make. Spend a little bit of money to have a professional design your site and make it look fantastic. You want a site that accurately presents you as a true professional.

As your business grows and you develop new products and services, you may want to build additional websites. For example, our NashvilleK9.com site is our main business, but we have developed others to serve the same or adjacent markets:

- <u>CoachFido.com</u> (online dog training school)
- <u>Pawdentity.com</u> (point-of-sale and kennel management software)
- <u>PetTaxxi.com</u> (pet transportation)
- <u>SecureAirCharter.net</u> (premier air charter)

Later in the book, I'll talk more about building your brand in order to perhaps sell it one day. Your website is part of your brand. Think carefully about the image you're projecting to the world, and don't be afraid to spend some money to make it look great.

After all, it's the way most people will be introduced to you and your business.

YOUR PERSONAL IMAGE

As you already know, the overriding theme in this book is the importance of personal relationships in building your business. Those relationships are built on trust, which depends in large part on people's perception that you're a true professional.

One of the most underrated ways to build your business is by investing in your personal image. I believe in presenting yourself to the public as a healthy, energetic, clean-cut pro.

For example, I usually shave on the days when I have in-person meetings. I'm a bit old-school, and my dad was a military guy who taught me the importance of being clean-cut and well put together. It's an important detail others see.

I feel that part of my image is presenting myself as a trim, healthy leader, so I work out five days a week and eat healthy most of the time.

If you're in good health, and you're physically fit, more people want to do business with you. They know that you take care of yourself, which requires discipline. If you can't tuck in your shirt, or if you're always out of breath because you're not in shape, that's less attractive.

I also "dress to impress," which is why I invest a significant amount of money in custom suits. If I have a meeting with someone, I'm not going to be underdressed. If I attend an event, I'm probably going to be one of the best-dressed people in the room.

In addition, I don't ever drink in public. I'm not a big drinker anyway, so that's not a major change from what I do in private. However, if I'm at an event, I won't drink because I don't want to compromise my judgment with alcohol.

There's no reason to risk my entire reputation because I drank too much at an event and said something stupid. That could be someone's last memory of me: Ali, the guy who drank too much and ran his mouth off.

At this stage of my life, it's not worth the risk.

I also feel I need to set an example for my children, colleagues, and employees. I have no judgment against people who drink at social events. It's just not my thing. That's why I practice discipline in this area.

When people think about "investing in your business," they typically think about money. As you can tell from this chapter, it's a lot more than that.

The very first place to invest is in yourself. If you do that consistently, along with taking action on the other items we've talked about in this chapter, you'll be ready to start getting the word out about your business. This is what we'll focus on in the following chapter.

CHAPTER FOUR

MARKET YOUR BUSINESS

Marketing can feel like heaven, or it can feel like hell.

Some business owners love marketing. They get excited about the creative aspects and enjoy learning about new technologies and opportunities to promote their business.

Other people absolutely hate marketing because they just want to "do the work." They see marketing as a necessary evil they have to endure in order to keep the lights on.

I implore you to take the first approach. You'll get much better results if you learn to enjoy marketing.

But remember, marketing *is* part of the work of your business. It's not a distraction. It's essential. In this chapter, I'm excited to share some thoughts on what I've learned about marketing.

FREE & LOW-COST MARKETING

Some of the very best marketing you will ever have doesn't cost a dime. What am I talking about? Reviews.

Whenever you have a client or customer who's pleased with you, ask them to leave a Google review. It's so simple, yet a lot of business owners neglect asking people for reviews.

When people need a service, what do they do? They do a Google search. It's the standard way we find businesses today. They're searching for every type of business under the sun: dog training, hairstyling, lawncare, chiropractic, you name it.

What are they looking for? They want someone who has a good reputation and delivers on what they promised. Your customer and client reviews can really help convince that person you're the one to solve their problem and to hire you.

You should also use the power of Google by attaching a Google Maps page (or a Yelp page) to your website.

In the last chapter, we talked about your website, which is an essential part of your business. I also recommend spending some money on a great logo. Unless you're a professional graphic designer, don't design your logo yourself.

Humans are visual creatures. Your logo speaks volumes about what you stand for. It's instantly recognizable. This is one area where you don't want to go for the cheapest option.

Once you have a great logo, use it everywhere. Not just on your website, but also on printed materials such as hats or shirts. You're going to put on clothes anyway. Why not market your business at the same time?

CREATIVE MARKETING

A good buddy of mine, Tyler Burnett, owns a company called Goat Turf, which makes artificial grass for indoor, outdoor, residential, and commercial use. One day we went to play golf and I gave him a hard time the whole day because his logo was literally on everything he wore or used.

His shirt was checkered with tiny versions of his logo. It was on the back of his golf clubs and embossed on his golf bag. His logo was on the towel he used to wipe down his golf balls and clubs. It was on everything.

When Tyler takes a client or prospect to the golf course, they see his logo everywhere. His enthusiasm for his logo might border on the excessive, but it works. When you spend nine or eighteen holes staring at a logo, it's going to be burned in your brain.

Tyler has done a great job thinking through the business application of his logo in a way that people will be exposed to it repeatedly over several hours.

SIMPLE BRANDING

Everyone thinks of branding and advertising as a billboard or an ad or TV or radio. They equate this with spending significant money.

Those avenues of promotion can be effective, but it's not practical when you're starting out— or maybe ever, depending on your business.

Branding can be as simple as using your logo or imagery on your clothing or vehicle.

We used to give away license plate frames that said, "My dog digs Nashville K-9." People loved them, and they cost around forty cents each.

Every car dealership uses this method of promotion. You can use it, too.

To cut costs, we started giving all our clients a Nashville K-9 decal. Surprisingly, lots of people put these on their cars, and decals are inexpensive to make.

These are just a few simple grassroots ways to market your business. You can always do things like social media ads, Google ads, and a hundred other ways to promote your business digitally. But there's something special about physical items that people love because they can touch them.

YOU ARE IN CONTROL

Remember that as an entrepreneur, you control your marketing and branding. You determine where your logo is placed, whether that's business cards, your website, shirts, decals, or other items.

We've done our best to make creative use of these items. One of the ways we've tried to stand out is by having a business card that feels like fur. It's very soft and feels different from any other business card out there.

When you flip it over, it lists all our pet-related businesses. Did it cost me a little more? Of course. But we are intentional about creating a luxurious feeling in everything we do and reminding people we're in the pet industry, even with something as simple as a business card.

Many years ago, there was another dog trainer in town who was almost a direct competitor. One of his promo videos on YouTube featured him handing a binder of instructions to a client after their visit. It was one of those binders from Office Depot where you hole-punch materials and slip a sheet of paper into the clear front cover.

I thought, *Are you kidding me?* I was astonished because we had all our materials pre-printed. Everywhere you look on the packet, you see our logo. It looks so much better than a homemade packet. You can see what I do when you get this book's bonuses at NashvilleK9.com/Discipline.

We still have all our client materials pre-printed to this day. It's one of many things that sets us apart from our competitors.

I recently saw an email that someone had sent our team. She was disappointed that the franchise owner didn't come and tell her "Hello" when she picked up her dog.

I was at the airport at the time, so I didn't have the chance to meet her. But I loved this message because it meant that our outfit looked so big and corporate that she thought it was a franchise.

I took her complaint as a compliment!

RELATIONSHIPS ARE THE BEST MARKETING

I've given you several ideas in this chapter about marketing and promotion. You can go crazy with tons of ideas to the point where you spend all your time chasing the latest trends.

To close this chapter, though, I want to bring you back to one of the bedrocks upon which we've built our business: relationships. You can have all the creative marketing in the world, but the very best marketing is great relationships with people.

Not too long ago, I hosted an inaugural fundraiser for the Make-A-Wish Foundation. We raised $180,000 in three hours with just thirty-seven couples donating.

I don't say that to boast but to point out that it wouldn't have been possible without spending years building relationships and connections with people who could donate an amount like this.

If you have a service-based business, all the creative marketing in the world won't save you from a lack of relationships. People eventually know whether you are there to serve the community, or whether you're there just to make money.

Logos, websites, business cards, swag, and Google reviews are all important. But the bedrock of your business is people. You don't have a business without them!

That's why in Part Two we will focus on how to serve people—specifically, your clients—by selling properly, doing the work with excellence, and teaching them what they need to be successful.

PART II

WORKING WITH CLIENTS

CHAPTER FIVE

SELL THE CLIENT

Summer brings all kinds of traditions for Americans: cookouts, the Fourth of July, water parks, and summer vacations.

For football fans, there's another tradition they get equally excited about: training camp.

Just like pro baseball players have spring training to get ready for the season, football players set aside time before their fall season kicks off.

Here in Nashville, people *love* the Tennessee Titans! Unlike baseball's spring training, where all the teams go to Florida (mostly due to weather concerns), football teams usually train close to home. For the Titans, that location is Saint Thomas Sports Park.

Training camp serves several purposes, including orienting new players to the team, helping veteran players get back in shape, and helping coaches establish the right tone and culture for the team.

But there's also another purpose for training camp: to revisit the fundamentals of the game. You might be able to run fast, be agile on your feet, or throw the ball a long distance.

But if you can't nail the fundamentals of the game, you're already dead in the water.

In the game of business, the most fundamental skill you can learn is *selling*. In this chapter, I'll walk you through my perspective on sales so you can continue growing your eventual seven-figure business.

YOU MUST LEARN HOW TO SELL

Selling is the lifeline of any business. If you look at the compensation different people in a larger business receive, who typically makes the most? That's right. It's the salesperson.

If you're selling suits, the sales guy is making more commission on the suit than the tailor or the person manufacturing the garment in a factory. Why is that?

It's because nothing works in a business if people don't buy the product or service. If you're working in a company and you aren't in sales, congrats. You probably don't have to worry about selling.

But since you're reading this book about what it really takes to build a seven-figure business, you can bet your life that selling is vital to your livelihood. Therefore, you must learn how to sell.

Read great sales books. Go to conferences. Do whatever it takes to become a great salesperson. In my industry, it doesn't do any good to be a really skilled dog trainer if you can't convince the person on the other end that they need your service.

Earlier in the book, we talked about the six pillars, which include being reliable, honest, and responsive. Those are all fundamental qualities of a good salesperson.

But they're not the whole picture. Let me share a perspective on a sales issue that many people today miss. It might be a bit controversial because we're not supposed to judge by appearances, right? But the truth is that we do.

APPEARANCE MATTERS

I'm a uniform person. I like people to tuck in their shirts, to be clean-cut, and for their clothes to be nice. That's important to me.

If you have a business where someone's wearing a uniform in public, and their shirt is tucked in, people will respect that more than if you have a guy in jeans with an untucked shirt. It's very important how you represent your brand to others.

One of my former managers at Nashville K-9 used to give me a lot of pushback on this. He wouldn't shave and looked scruffy all the time. He also didn't want to tuck in his shirt and didn't like me asking him to do that.

This is a basic principle of professionalism. I'm constantly surprised how many people don't care about looking their best on the job.

When you see pictures of people at work in earlier generations, like the 1920s through the 1950s, how did they look? They dressed up. Even when people were out having fun or spending time with their families, they looked sharp.

If you see people in bread lines from the 1920s, many of those gentlemen were wearing suits! They embraced the discipline of looking sharp even in the most difficult circumstances.

I'm not suggesting that every industry requires a suit. But a professional appearance makes a huge difference in how the customer perceives your quality of service.

There's a reason that Chick-fil-A is one of the most popular and successful fast-food franchises in the country. Although their food is good, that's not the whole explanation for their success. When you go through the Chick-fil-A drive-thru, you're greeted by young people who look sharp and have great attitudes.

The level of professionalism makes a big difference!

Here's another example. I have a Mercedes and sometimes need to have it serviced. There are two dealerships near my office.

The first is five minutes away. When you go through their service bay, you're greeted by a guy with poofy hair sticking out from underneath a hat. He's wearing jeans, an untucked shirt, and ratty tennis shoes.

The second one is twenty-five minutes away. When you visit the service bay, you're greeted by a service guy wearing slacks and a nice Mercedes shirt that's tucked in. He's not wearing a hat and is clean-cut.

Which dealership do you think I prefer? That's right—the one with the more professional-looking service guy.

The slogan of Mercedes-Benz is "The best or nothing." Yet if I drive to the service area with the guy who doesn't look like a professional, am I getting the best or nothing? I feel like I'm getting nothing right off the bat.

Every encounter with your customer or client, or potential customer or client, is an opportunity to sell. Are you going to give them a reason to continue working with you? Your appearance is a big part of this equation.

TWO KEY PARTS OF SALES

Countless books and resources have been created to help people learn how to sell. I don't need to recreate a list here. Instead, let me give you a quick summary of a few critical parts of selling.

Obviously, the first part of selling is figuring out who your prospects are. What are they like? Where are they located? What is their income level? What are their needs, fears, interests, and concerns?

When you're thinking about your prospects, it's important to qualify them first. It doesn't do any good to spend time trying to sell to people who aren't the right fit for your service.

At Nashville K-9, we serve clients who can afford elite dog training. Therefore, we don't target people who are worried about paying for this month's groceries.

The second part of selling is figuring out how to contact those prospects. This will depend hugely on what kind of business you have, so suffice it to say that you need to figure out where those people exist, either geographically or online, and then find ways to reach them.

Once you know whom you're trying to reach and how to reach them, then you must understand how to talk about your product or service in a way that appeals to them.

This is where knowing the four personality types of prospects comes in handy.

THE FOUR PERSONALITIES OF PROSPECTS

Most sales books talk about prospects as if people fall into one singular category. The problem with that approach is that it doesn't take different personalities into account.

There was a study that identified four main groups of people. Let me break it down quickly.

The **accountant** is a highly detailed person who focuses on features, functions, facts, and logic. Engineers, CPAs, and architects fall into this category.

The **entertainer** loves people. They enjoy throwing events and parties and will sit down next to you at the bar to strike up a conversation. An entertainer is not a wallflower. Just like my son, they will woo you immediately.

The **fighter** is a type A person who needs to get things done. They hate it when people waste their time. They live to make quick decisions, then drive on. Most CEOs and business owners are fighters.

The **counselor** likes to take in all the information but needs to take a couple of days to process it and decide before getting back to you.

As a seller, you need to change your approach depending on who you're talking to.

The accountant doesn't want you to ask what they did over the weekend. If you're helping them close a loan, they want to know the closing costs, the interest rates, and the time frame. Any irrelevant information is a waste of time for them.

The entertainer, however, doesn't care about any of those things. They want you to ask about their family and what they did over the weekend. They want to build rapport with you and don't care much about the interest rate as long as they like and trust you.

The fighter is a hard close. You can't dillydally with them. They don't care what you did over the weekend. The facts and figures have some importance to them, but more than anything, they want to feel like they've "won" and then close the interaction so they can move on.

The counselor is going to take a couple of days to deliberate. They will probably ask others for their input. But once they're committed, they're in.

People come in all shapes, sizes, and personalities. When you're selling, try to identify the personality of your prospect, then adjust your sales technique. That's part of the craft and fun of selling.

CLOSING THE SALE

Naturally, many of your prospects will have questions and objections. I don't have the space here to detail an entire list of how to handle objections, but my main advice would be to keep a list of all the objections people raise as you encounter them.

The more you sell, the more objections and questions you will hear. As you become more seasoned as a seller, and your confidence grows, you'll be able to address these in your conversations.

Then, the most important part of the whole process is actually closing the sale. At Nashville K-9, it might go something like this:

"Okay, Susie, we've talked about all the needs you have for dog training. I have this Tuesday or Thursday available. Which day is better for you to drop off your dog?"

"Let me think about it for a moment. I think Thursday will work."

"Great. Would you like 8:00 a.m. or 10:00 a.m.?"

"I like to sleep in. I'll take 10:00 a.m."

Boom, then you're closed. Notice that the first question wasn't "Hi, Susie, when would you like to bring in your dog?" Susie will have to think about it, talk to her family, and then may or may not get back to you.

A big part of selling is leading the client and being decisive. When you ask open-ended questions about when they are available to do this or that, it leaves an open loop.

Your job is to close the loop. In doing so, you'll have a much better chance of closing the sale.

And once you close the sale, it's time to do the work they've hired you to do. That's the topic of the next chapter.

CHAPTER SIX

DO THE WORK

Whatever business you're in, you have sold the client on the value you're providing. Now, you have to fulfill that obligation.

If you have a service-based business and you're charging a higher price than your competitors, you have to build the value to justify the higher price. Your pricing should be commensurate with the time you've taken to invest in your vocation.

Maybe you've attended all the best seminars and training. Maybe you've traveled the country learning from mentors.

That's great, but what actually moves the needle? That's right, it's being disciplined and getting the work done.

You promised the client you would train their dog seven days a week, multiple times a day. Then you need to deliver. You're ethically obligated to them since they're paying you for all the things you've committed to do.

IT'S SIMPLE YET DIFFICULT

"Do the work" sounds simple, even juvenile. I mean, isn't it obvious you have to show up and do the work you promised?

You'd think so. But lots of people will go to great lengths to cut corners or make excuses for why they couldn't deliver on a promise.

It goes back to one of the core pillars of business we talked about in Chapter One. You have to be honest and reliable. If you're not, guess what? The clients and customers who didn't get what they paid for will tell all their friends, and your business will go down the toilet.

Sure, creative marketing can help business. But over the long term, what really helps your business grow is fulfilling your obligations to your clients and allowing them to tell other people via word of mouth, testimonials, reviews, and referrals.

It's not always easy to do the work and follow through on your commitments.

You don't feel like putting in the work when it's ninety degrees outside, and you're getting crushed by the sun. You've done it with five dogs already, but you have to keep going.

It's hard when it's raining, and the dogs don't want to be out in the rain because they're pets, but you have to work with them.

It's a pain when it's cold and snowy, but the dogs need to go outside and eliminate. They can't do it themselves.

It's definitely not fun when a dog has an accident. Maybe it's a puppy in their kennel or on their run. You have to remove them, bathe them, disinfect the run, dry it off, and put it back in place.

Sound like fun? It's not. It's horrible. But the secret to getting through it is that you've got to get comfortable being uncomfortable. You must have a "whatever it takes" mentality. You are obligated to that person who commissioned you to fulfill the value you promised when you sold them.

You need to take that responsibility very seriously. If you do, they will, too. Not only that, they will also refer you and help build your business. But it's up to you to set the standard.

GET USED TO THE SUCK

I don't want to sound melodramatic, but for years, it was miserable running Nashville K-9. I trained myself to put up with it because I was making some money. It wasn't a lot of money at the time, but I was grateful for it.

In order to grow the business and buy a Chevy Tahoe, I kept reinvesting my profits. After I bought the Tahoe, I was able to buy a dog trailer and, after that, a property that could house the dogs. This is how my business evolution went.

I was doing loans, being a police officer, serving with search and rescue when called upon, and doing public demonstrations until the public got tired of seeing me. I was training dog after dog, closing loan after loan, and spending any free time I had announcing it with marketing.

People see my business now, with our amazing facility and my private jet, and they want what I have. But they didn't see the years and years of getting used to the suck and unexplainable difficulty of making it happen day by day.

I remember one Christmas in particular. I had one employee at the time and had completely gutted my garage to build cinderblock kennels with chain link fencing. My neighborhood wasn't zoned for this, but I did it anyway. My makeshift kennel could hold twenty-eight dogs.

My employee quit at Christmas, and I had all these dogs overlapping into Christmas and New Year's. Every time a dog had an accident, even if it was 2:30 a.m., my wife would kick me out of bed, and I'd have to take care of it.

This meant I had to let the dog out, wash the dog, then wash the run because the smell would permeate through the whole house. Then I'd bring the dog back in.

I also had two dogs that a friend of mine asked me to watch because he was going out of town. One of the dogs had stress diarrhea, and the mess would get all over the other dog because they were in the same run.

This happened every day I had those dogs. I bathed them multiple times a day and cleaned their kennel. This was the last time those dogs were allowed over!

All told, during that time, I had twenty-eight dogs in my care. I had to train them, exercise them, feed them, let them eliminate, and do everything else required to make sure they were cared for.

I did all of "the suck" work by myself for a long, long time. I have a great appreciation for true entrepreneurs who are putting in the grind. For example, somebody who has a food truck has to prepare all the food. They also must clean the truck, drive to different places, keep the truck in working order, and fill it with gas. Then, add to that all of the financial aspects of a business.

I appreciate that person because I know the suck. I understand how hard it is to be disciplined and get things done.

You have to convince yourself this is part of the deal. Once you do, and you realize that it's part of building a business, you get comfortable with the suck.

I can tell you that it sucks when you're washing a dog and you get their pee or poop in your mouth when it sprays on you. It gets all over your clothes, and you smell like poop or pee all day. Doesn't get any better than that!

But I got through it because I realized the suck was part of the journey.

ARE YOU PUTTING IN THE HOURS?

It's not just about "the suck," it's also about putting in the time. One of the big distinguishing features of people who are successful and those who aren't is the amount of time they have dedicated to their craft.

Look at Tony Robbins. He's put over ten thousand hours into his speaking career. Why do people pay Tony Robbins a fortune to go to his seminars? Because he's world-class at what he does.

Or what about Jerry Seinfeld? As a comedian, he's adamant about telling people he's a real professional, not just someone who got lucky. It takes him a long time to develop a stand-up routine and deliver it in a way that the punchlines are perfect.

When Seinfeld made his first appearance on Johnny Carson's *Tonight Show* in 1981, he rehearsed his stand-up routine two hundred times! And his work ethic has never wavered through the years.

If you watch the early seasons of *Seinfeld* compared to the later seasons, you can clearly see how he matured as an actor and how his delivery improved. Jerry Seinfeld is probably at a genius level compared to most other comedians.

If you want to succeed in any field, you have to put in the work. You have to practice your craft. As a comedian, you have to do sets at every dumpy club and perform at 2:00 a.m. in weird places when nobody's watching. You do this because you have to see what's funny.

In other words, you've got to put in the reps.

Everybody wants the magic potion, the easy button, the quick solution. But it doesn't exist, at least not for professionals who want to rise to the pinnacle of success.

POSITION YOURSELF TO BE LUCKY

At this point, you're getting the message that building a million-dollar business isn't easy.

When I had those twenty-eight dogs, I still had to email pictures, make videos of the dogs, market the business on social media, and mess with the website. There was so much to do that I basically lived, breathed, and ate the business to get to where I am now.

People don't realize how hard it is. It's cumbersome and labor-intensive, and the stress is always on your mind.

What they think now is *Oh, Ali's got a cool jet and drives a Ferrari. He's so lucky.* Sure, a bit of luck may be a part of it. I'll give you that. But you have to position yourself to be lucky. It doesn't just happen out of the blue.

You must be ready to seize those opportunities when they come.

I don't know of any millionaires who didn't work their tails off. Sure, you'll see a fluke every once in a while, maybe a Bitcoin guy who accidentally became an overnight sensation.

But even the people who are social media influencers are working eight to ten hours a day, thinking of clever memes and videos to inspire and entertain their audience.

They make it look easy when they take pictures of themselves inside a private jet, but it took a ton of videos for them to get inside that jet.

Here's what's great about America: this is the land of freedom. It's capitalistic. You can come here with no degree and make yourself into somebody. There aren't a lot of other countries where that's possible.

I'll always be grateful for the opportunities given to me. But I didn't do it alone. Lots of people helped me recognize and take advantage of those opportunities.

One of those people was my mentor, Denny Elliot, who is a perfect example of *doing the work.*

FROM INSTRUCTOR TO ENTREPRENEUR

When I became involved in law enforcement, one of the first things I noticed was something interesting. Some officers spend their whole careers basically doing a singular job, while others look for opportunities in their department to advance themselves.

I first met Denny when I joined the Williamson County Sheriff's Office. As a SWAT operator, you have to keep yourself in top physical shape because you are basically the 911 for the police.

Denny was the training instructor for the department and had been with the department for many years. As my lieutenant and former SWAT team leader, he held himself to an even higher standard of excellence.

But he didn't just meet the standards. He exceeded them on every level. Denny wasn't just a trainer. He was also a practitioner of everything he taught us.

Denny was there to make sure the men and women under his care came home at night. He truly cared about helping others stay safe and be successful.

He was also a true academic who would study the books and run ballistics tests himself. In addition, he was an instructor for the International Association of Law Enforcement Firearms Instructors.

In other words, Denny put in the work so he could be the best of the best.

After he retired from law enforcement, Denny decided to parlay his skills into a training business. Today, he travels across the country and abroad as the foremost sniper instructor for police departments.

As a police officer, Denny was likely making around $60,000 per year with an annual pay bump of 1–2 percent. Today, he runs a very successful business impacting police departments and saving countless lives in the process.

All because he chose to *do the work*.

These results aren't unique to him. You can also position yourself through hard work to take advantage of the opportunities right in front of you.

Do that long enough, and one day you can have your own multimillion-dollar empire.

CHAPTER SEVEN

TEACH THE CLIENT

What's the ultimate goal of a business? Is it to

- Make money?
- Build your reputation?
- Give your family a better future?
- Provide a flexible schedule?

Yes, a business can give you all those things and more. But at its heart, a business only exists for one reason: *to solve a problem for the client or customer.*

A restaurant solves the problem of being hungry. A lawncare business solves the problem of an unsightly yard. A plumber solves the problem of clogged-up pipes. A chiropractor solves the problem of misalignment in your spine. And so on.

Your relationship with your client or customer doesn't exist just during the transaction. It extends far beyond that, or at least it should.

You can solve their immediate problem when you provide your product or service. But how can you help them in an ongoing way after you have done your part?

You do this by teaching the client. The best business leaders are not just creators or service providers. They are also teachers who do everything they can to ensure their clients' success.

A LITTLE BACKGROUND

Let me set some context for how we approach this at Nashville K-9.

In the last chapter, we talked about doing the work. One of the ways we do that is by training every dog at least three times a day. We also exercise them eight to ten times a day. In addition, we work on behavioral issues twice daily with a rotation between all our trainers.

On Tuesdays and Saturdays, we email the client twenty or more pictures of their dog so they can see we're doing the work. That way, they are able to keep up with the dog's training progress.

Four or five days before the client picks up their dog, we also email them a video of their dog in action. The video creates value for the client, but it's also insurance for us.

The client could always come back and say, "My dog didn't know to do this or that." Then, we can show them a video of their dog doing that exact thing.

While it doesn't happen very often, occasionally, a client will make an accusation or an allegation that we didn't do our part. The video proves we did.

OUR CLIENT TRAINING PROCESS

When we train the client, we spend about half an hour going over the routine. It's optimized around a normal person's workday.

It would be much more convenient for us to hand the client written instructions. But we have found that it makes it easier for the client to go through the routine. Most people are rule followers and can easily follow our instructions to let the dog out to use the bathroom at a certain time in the morning, train them at this time, feed them at this time, etc.

On pickup/graduation day, we review dog psychology with the client. We also review operant conditioning and classical conditioning so they understand the reason our training has worked. In addition, we do a Q&A time, give them a packet of information from trusted partners, and hand them a coupon for future boarding.

Then, we take the client and their dog to the field, where we do a command and have them do it as well. We go back and forth until they feel comfortable with the dog, going through each command one by one.

Once they've completed that, we snap a picture of the dog wearing a mortarboard hat alongside the owner, in front of our step/repeat banner on the red carpet to complete the graduation process. The dog has been trained to the standards we set, and they've graduated! (You'll want to see our exceptionally cute graduates! Check them out on Instagram: @NashvilleK9.)

Post-graduation, they go home with a tutorial video of the training we've taken them through. They also have access to our online training site, CoachFido.com.

That's a quick summary of the support we offer to clients to help them succeed after we send the dog home with them. They can always call us if they have an issue, and we can schedule a time to remedy the problem.

CLEAR COMMUNICATION IS ESSENTIAL

A question I often get about our training is "Do you guarantee your training?" I'd estimate that 70 percent of our clients ask this.

My answer is "We guarantee standing behind our training, provided the client continues the training on their own." We take this approach so there is no misunderstanding of what we're there to provide them with in the future. We have learned these lessons by servicing clients for many years.

One time, we had a client who basically wanted a free week of training by making allegations that we hadn't done our training correctly. We went ahead and did the week of training out of goodwill. However, I knew she only did this because she wanted to go out of town and didn't want to pay to board the dog somewhere.

You learn along the way that people are fickle, and sometimes they'll try to take advantage of you.

As a result, you have to be very precise with your wording on what they're going to get. We take great pains to communicate to clients specifically what we're providing, so much so that we email a packet of info with every little detail of the training, even before they pay a deposit.

Don't assume that clients know what basic terms mean. You know the ins and outs of your industry, but they probably don't.

For example, what does "sit" mean? "Sit" means that a dog sits in a position and remains there for generally thirty or more feet as you walk away. Then you come back and reward the dog.

In our three-week program, "sit" can mean 80–200 feet, but it's spelled out precisely for the client so they can't come back and say, "I didn't know this or that was going to happen." They sign an agreement, but the packet is another layer of understanding and communication that articulates every single command.

This may seem like over-communication. But there's really no such thing as over-communicating, especially when you're doing a service for people. It's important to do this so everything is spelled out in black and white, no one misrepresents themselves, and the client understands (and gets) what they paid for.

This is how we teach our clients at Nashville K-9. Although our business is dog training, you can take these same principles and use them for your clients and customers.

What videos, packets, training, answers, routines, or other resources can you give your customers to help them succeed after they have finished their work with you?

PART III

SCALING FOR GROWTH

CHAPTER EIGHT

FOLLOW-UP CONSISTENTLY

At this point in your journey, you've laid the foundation, you've sold to clients, and you have income flowing because you're doing the work. Now it's time to begin scaling for long-term growth.

It might seem a little strange that I've included a chapter on follow-up here in Part Three, where we're talking about scaling. Wouldn't a chapter on follow-up belong in Part Two, where we were talking about working with clients?

Yes and no. Follow-up is part of client work, but I've included this chapter in Part Three because it's a key part of scaling your business. Many business owners don't do a good job with follow-up. But the ones who do will see much faster growth.

Just like caffeine helps you get moving on a sluggish morning, follow-up will supercharge your business. You won't get to seven figures without it. Hence, my inclusion of follow-up here in Part Three as we're talking about scaling.

REVENUE RECAPTURE

In Chapter Seven, we talked about teaching the client what they need to be successful after you've done the work. It's a great opportunity to create goodwill with the client and set a wonderful tone for a long-term relationship with them.

But you don't want the good vibes to end there. Make sure to follow up consistently, not only because it's the thoughtful and generous thing to do but also because it's great for business.

Follow-up is a great chance to recapture more revenue from the client or customer. Not just because you want to make more money, but because you can add more value to the client.

One very simple thing you can do in following up is offer a more advanced version of what you've already sold them. In the dog training world, we offer advanced training as another way we can serve them (and also get paid more).

You can also use follow-up as an opportunity for retail sales. For example, we use Merrick pet food at Nashville K-9. I have chosen not to sell dog food in our facility because it's a hassle to deal with all the tax paperwork for the state. But if I wanted to be a retailer, I could easily say, "Come in and grab your next bag of dog food from us."

Or we could also offer a delivery service. "We'll be happy to bring you X number of bags." We could also add items like training supplies, treats, leashes, collars, and more.

Remember, though, that selling is not the first thing you should be doing when you follow up. Your first concern should be asking questions like

- How is your dog doing?

- Do you have any questions about the training?

- Can we do anything to improve our relationship?

Once you have shown the client that you care about how they're doing, then you can mention other items. "Don't forget that next month is fall break, and we're filling up pretty quickly. Let's go ahead and get you scheduled." Or, "If you're interested, we have some items for sale to complement your training."

Business is all about an exchange of value. Everything you do should be geared toward adding value to the client, not just making the sale.

FOLLOW-UP TIMING

This might be a good opportunity to share a bit about our follow-up process.

We have a set follow-up schedule where we contact the client a total of five times after we have trained their dog:

- Ten days
- One month
- Three months
- Six months
- One year

After one year, we don't do regular follow-ups, but they do get a Christmas card from us. It's a fine line because you want to follow up regularly, but you don't want to be a pest about it.

We have clients we've converted to ongoing revenue through more training or occasional tune-ups for their dog. We don't contact these clients on the schedule I just mentioned because they're already here.

But we are persistent and disciplined in contacting the clients who aren't here after their initial training. They know we're not running and hiding from them. We make it clear that we're here to serve them, and they're on our minds.

It might not convert into regular revenue right then or even within the next year. However, maybe they have another dog, or their friend or neighbor has a dog that needs to be trained.

Great follow-up is vital, but it's become a lost art. Which is unfortunate because it doesn't take that much effort.

REVIEWS AND REFERRALS

A final item to include in your follow-up is asking for reviews and referrals. Many people don't think of this, but it can make a huge difference for your business.

If a client is happy with your service, ask them to leave a Google review for your business. If you wait too long, they won't remember as much about your service. So, ask right away. You can also use the review on your website.

There are various ways you can ask for referrals, but my suggestion is to keep things simple. At the same time you ask for a review, ask the client if they know anyone who might also enjoy your service. You could even give them a coupon, discount, or some other incentive that encourages the client to send their friends and family your way.

You've already put the work into building your business. When you follow up intentionally, you can supercharge your success by letting your clients and their network support you as well.

CHAPTER NINE

REINVEST YOUR PROFITS

Business owners are prone to making lots of mistakes. And for good reason—because we're all growing and learning. And with growth comes mistakes.

By definition, with each stage of growth, you're entering into new territory. You're heading into uncharted waters, which means everything is new. Mistakes are going to happen.

One of the most common mistakes I see business owners make is not reinvesting their profits back into their business. Once you've worked for years to build your business and you have a good income, it's easy to level off and simply coast.

I caution you not to do that. Sure, you can stay at a comfortable level your whole life. Many, if not most, business owners do this exact thing. But if you want to have a seven-figure business that is always on an upward trajectory, you can't stay where you are.

Perhaps the best way to illustrate this is by sharing how I kept investing in Nashville K-9. I'm not saying I did everything perfectly, but it's a good illustration of how to keep growing over the long term.

THE EARLY YEARS

In the early years of Nashville K-9, I had a townhouse apartment where I kept eight dogs, all in crates in the bedroom. I'd have to drive back and forth, back and forth, to run and train the dogs.

Then we upgraded to a home in the Green Hills part of Nashville. I gutted the basement and built kennels, which was awesome since I then had a place to store the dogs on a more permanent basis.

We built drains into the floors and had a grinder pump, so if we needed to wash the dogs or they eliminated, everything would go down through the pump into the sewage system. None of this was allowed by the municipal code. I just had people come and do it because it was necessary for my business.

At this time, I was still using my Chevy Tahoe and a dog trailer. Once I had space in my new place, I went from around eight dogs to twenty or twenty-five at a time.

I would drive to the training field I leased, train and exercise the dogs, load them back in and drive home, then switch them out with the next crew. I had an assistant, but he quit right before Christmas one year, as I mentioned in a previous chapter.

Around this same, I was driving to the training field one day, and two deer ran into the side of my car. It really put me in a pickle because body shops were closed during the holidays. That meant my Tahoe would be stuck in the shop for about a month, so I walked the dogs around the neighborhood instead.

SEVEN ACRES OF FREEDOM

After that happened, I told my wife, "This area is getting pretty congested, and the town is catching on to what I'm doing." It wasn't really legal to operate a business, especially a kennel, out of your house. It was a gray area because the code didn't address running a kennel from your home.

Nevertheless, I knew I was on shaky ground and that I was at risk of being sued by the city if they decided to pursue the matter. As a result, we started looking for farms. We eventually bought an equestrian farm in Franklin that was a little over seven acres.

We converted the barn into kennels, added two air-conditioning units, and insulated the attic with spray foam. We also added a gun range on the property. I had never made an investment this big into my business, but I felt a freedom I'd never known before since we had lots of space.

We were there for seven years. At the time, the investment was a huge deal for me, but it really paid off because it allowed the business to grow significantly.

LITTLE SURPRISES

Having more space meant I was able to handle more dogs, which meant that more revenue was coming in. That allowed us to keep on improving the property with items like fencing and a solar array. At that time, people were very big on green initiatives. It was good for business because I could then tell people we were a "green" company.

In full transparency, though, it was not worth it. Although the solar panels did help offset some costs of electricity, in the end, it did not make financial sense.

That's just one example of the surprises you have when you invest in property. You have to keep the long-term vision in mind when unexpected expenses and issues arise.

For example, the farm was used by the previous owners to train horses. This meant the ground was full of divots that could easily twist a client's ankle. As a result, we had to invest in someone to come out and level out the ground.

We also discovered that Tennessee is built on rocks, so you have constant issues with needing to have rocks removed. You learn a lot when you buy property and want to improve it, but it's simply a part of investing in your business.

AUTO-ATTENDANTS AND AUTO-FLEETS

It's not all about the big things like buying farms, putting up fencing, or hiring people to level the ground on your property. Sometimes, the little investments in your business make a huge difference.

For the longest time, I carried around two phones—one for business and one for personal use. The business phone would ring at all hours of the day and night. There's nothing like getting a call at 9:00 p.m. from someone who has a question about dog training.

After I read *The 4-Hour Work Week* by Tim Ferriss, I took his advice to create an auto-attendant. The purpose was to tell people you weren't available but would call them back at a certain time.

This was life-changing because it set the expectation that if I missed a call, I would call the person back. I was no longer tied to the phone and could call them back at my convenience.

My life was more manageable, and I looked more professional. Little things can do that, but big things can as well.

As the business grew, we added a few cars to the fleet and a side-by-side all-terrain vehicle. When you have two or three trainers going out at once, especially if the branded cars are in a row, it makes your organization look bigger. People assume you have fifty cars in the fleet.

We started doing more public events because the free publicity was very helpful. We did an event at the Adventure Science Center in Nashville, where we brought in working dogs. The kids and parents were captivated, which led to us appearing on a local TV show for kids that aired on the Fox station every Saturday.

When lots of people see you on TV, it has a spiraling effect that allows you to position yourself to seize more opportunities and open doors that are presented to you. We were also listed as a partner on the museum's website, which was great for business.

These are the kinds of opportunities that investing in your business can bring. When you put in the time and sweat equity, you can build a grassroots campaign that gives you organic marketing and word of mouth.

That's the best kind of marketing. This kind of disciplined, consistent public relations (PR) pays huge dividends in helping you scale your business. It's the difference between building a business and building a long-term brand.

CHAPTER TEN

BUILD TO SELL

We're nearing the end of the journey!

I'm so grateful to have the opportunity to come alongside you on your quest to build a seven-figure business. Thanks for entrusting me as your guide.

We've focused on building your business on a firm foundation, followed by educating yourself and not just investing in your business, but marketing as well.

Then, we spent some time talking through how to work with clients. I shared lots of specifics on selling your services to your clients, doing the work they've paid you to do, and teaching them what they need to know in order to be successful.

In the last two chapters, I've encouraged you to scale your business by consistently following up with clients and reinvesting your profits to ensure continued growth.

That's a lot of ground to cover. But we're not quite finished yet. In this chapter, I want to challenge you to think bigger by building your business to sell to someone else.

THINKING LONG-TERM

When you're in the thick of building your business, it's not easy to think long-term. As I've already discussed at length, I spent many years being consumed by the day-to-day demands of running Nashville K-9 as a solo business owner.

The same will be true for you. Unless you're independently wealthy from the get-go, you'll also spend a good length of time building up your business through your own efforts. It's hard to think long-term when you're consumed by the hundreds of things you've got to accomplish that day just to keep the lights on.

I challenge you to not be "normal" in the way you think about your business. Most people are just trying to get through the day. But what if you planned on selling your business right from the beginning? How would that change things?

Don't just build a business. Build a brand instead.

A brand is a sellable business. I can leave Nashville K-9, and it will still have its own identity. If I had called it "Ali's K-9," guess what? Then, people would always be expecting Ali to be involved.

It's pretty hard to sell a business if your name is tied to it. Most people don't give a lot of consideration to their business name, but I challenge you to use one that's not tied to you personally.

Also, be careful about giving your business a name that's tied to a specific location. To be honest, I have regretted naming my business "Nashville K-9" because I didn't consider that I might want to create a franchise one day.

If I decided to expand, I could always call it "Chicago K-9" or "Memphis K-9" or something similar. If I could go back in time, I wouldn't tie my business name to Nashville.

BE AN OUTLIER

You might feel like resisting my advice in this chapter if you're running the show by yourself right now. But I want you to think five, ten, or twenty years down the road.

I didn't write this book for people who think small. I wrote it for people who want to be enormously successful, who want to be an outlier in their field and dominate their industry. That's why you can't think small and tie your name to your business.

You may not have heard of Richard Schulze, but I guarantee you've heard of his company.

He was a rep for a company that made components for electronics before he opened up a little stereo equipment shop called Sound of Music in 1966. Later, he renamed it Best Buy, which grew into a massive chain of electronics stores.

Schultze had the wisdom to avoid naming his store Schultze's Stereo Equipment or something similar. He also had the wisdom to improve upon his original name, Sound of Music, because people are interested in more than just music equipment.

Bonus points because Best Buy is short and catchy!

If you want to be an outlier, think long-term. Sure, you can create a business that makes you a couple hundred thousand dollars a year, and that's fine.

But if you want to grow to seven figures and beyond, think bigger. It's not just about you and your income. You have to build it in a way that you can eventually step out of it.

This means not just thinking like an owner, but also a person who trains, delegates, and equips others to succeed.

Entire books have been written on those topics, and I don't have the space to dive into them here. But for now, I want to challenge you to think far beyond your day-to-day tasks that consume you in the early years of your business. What could the future hold for you?

SOME CONSIDERATIONS FOR SERVICE-BASED BUSINESSES

If you are considering selling at some point, you need to bring in a business-minded person to help ensure that you sell your business for what it's worth.

If you have this type of business and you've been working in it for a few decades, you may have reached the age when you're tired and are looking forward to retirement. I've seen it many times: the founder is itching to get out from under the business, and they are too quick to cut bait and run.

You see this a lot with veterinarians. They work on building a successful practice their whole life, but in general, they're not businesspeople. They don't really enjoy the hassle of payroll, marketing, and the business side of things. They just want to be practitioners.

What happens then? They sell their business to a bigger company for a ridiculously low multiple. Then, they stay on a couple of days a week over the next year to ensure a smooth transition.

The investor has purchased their company, knowing that the owner's emotional state is frail. Yet they also know the business is on an upswing. So, they come in with better processes and software to optimize the business.

This happens with service-based businesses of many kinds, including lots of medical practitioners and physicians. Be careful not to undervalue your business. My best advice would be to consult with good businesspeople so a savvier investor doesn't take advantage of you.

SUCCESS BEGINS NOW

We've covered a lot of ground in this book. In a relatively small amount of space, you've learned why discipline is the most important element in building a seven-figure business.

You might be tempted to set aside this book and think about its lessons for a while. Let me encourage you not to do that. Instead, I challenge you to *take action right now.* Don't wait.

The single biggest factor in your success is your ability to act on what you have learned. Don't procrastinate. Don't wait for the perfect time. It will never come.

All you have is today. Put what I've taught you into practice, and you'll be well on your way to building the business of your dreams.

All it takes is discipline.

RECOMMENDED BOOKS

In Chapter Two, you learned about the importance of educating yourself. If you want to build discipline into your life and grow a seven-figure business, these books are a great place to start:

How to Win Friends and Influence People by Dale Carnegie

Blink, *Outliers*, and *The Tipping Point* by Malcolm Gladwell

Inspire Greatness by Matt Tenney

Rich Dad Poor Dad by Robert Kiyosaki

Think and Grow Rich by Napoleon Hill

The Power of Positive Thinking by Norman Vincent Peale

PLEASE REVIEW THIS BOOK

If you enjoyed this book, would you take a few moments to leave a review wherever you purchased it (and perhaps even Goodreads. com)? I'm grateful for your support. Thank you!

GRATITUDE

I have eternal gratitude for my clients. They have entrusted me with their family member to not only accomplish our goals but to also care for them as if they were my own.

Most importantly, I'm grateful to my wife for always having my back, no matter what. Thank you for proofreading, commenting, suggesting, sacrificing, and encouraging. My wife is the best. She cares about me, and she wants the family to persevere.

Thank you to my mother and father. My father died ten days before I graduated from high school, but he couldn't have built two other better men than my brother and me.

My mother has done nothing but encourage, support, care, be involved, shove, and love me. I work to make sure my mother and father are proud that their sacrifices were not in vain. As Andy Stanley once said, "Your most important contribution to God's kingdom may not be something you do, but someone you raise."

Serial Entrepreneur, Pilot, Triathlete, and Philanthropist

BOOK ALI TO SPEAK!

Book Ali as your Keynote Speaker and you're guaranteed to inspire and motivate your audience!

For more info—visit AliHemyari.com

WHO IS ALI HEMYARI?

Ali Hemyari is a serial entrepreneur who started various businesses, from advertising to becoming a pet industry expert. He's a multi-event triathlete, a helicopter and airplane pilot, a real estate guru, a certified SWAT Operator, a Sniper/Firearms Instructor, and a general try-hard, servant-hearted, overachiever who wants to make a difference in today's world.

He's a husband and father, a God seeker, and an overall inspiring leader who hopes that his story can effect a significant change in someone who wants to be better, do more, accomplish, and help.

Ali is also a philanthropist who loves humans. He hopes that his path can inspire others to do more, break their personal barriers and goals, and live a Godly life.

Visit https://hemyaricompanies.com to learn more and see a complete list of his companies.

www.ingramcontent.com/pod-product-compliance
Lightning Source LLC
Chambersburg PA
CBHW051630120626
46551CB00014B/2021